Pocahontas

Princess of the River Tribes

To our godchild, Nicolas, whose ancestors were among
those Native Americans who were the first to see the "Tall Ships."

0-590-44372-0

12 11 10 9 8 7 6 5 4 3 2 1   3 4 5 6 7 8/9

Printed in the U.S.A.   08

First Scholastic printing, September 1993

Pocahontas

Princess of the River Tribes

by Elaine Raphael and Don Bolognese

Cartwheel
·B·O·O·K·S· ™
Scholastic Inc.
New York Toronto London Auckland Sydney

Pocahontas

Pocahontas was a princess,
daughter of the great chief, Powhatan.
Every day she played with her brothers
and sisters.
She ran through the woods and she swam
in the river that flowed past her village.

She could turn cartwheels faster than anyone
and she could climb the highest trees.
One morning she stood on the branch of a tall pine.
"I am like the eagle," she sang to the sun.
"I can see everything — even the great water,
the sea that never ends."

Powhatan

On a fall day, Powhatan took Pocahontas upriver
to visit one of his villages.
They passed silent oak forests and tall grassy marshes.
As the village came into view, Pocahontas heard singing.
It was a song about her father.
The people were singing, "Welcome, Great Chief,
ruler of all the river tribes."

The People

The people greeted them with honor.
They gave many gifts to Powhatan.
The great chief picked out a bright copper headband
and placed it on his daughter's head, saying:

"This comes from the earth, but shines like the sun. Only a chief's daughter can wear this. All who see it will know that you are a princess."

The Winter Hunt

In winter the river tribes moved inland to hunt.
Pocahontas helped her mother preserve the deer meat
and prepare the hides.
She learned to paint on deerskin and make pictures
with seashells and porcupine quills.
At day's end, while her mother softly chanted the evening song,
Pocahontas watched the sun fall behind the faraway hills.
One night her mother gave her a soft leather pouch.
"This is for your most precious things," she whispered.
Pocahontas fell asleep holding her deerskin pouch.
In it was her copper headband.

The Dance

The winter hunt was over.
The tribe held a big feast.
Pocahontas was chosen to dance at the celebration.
Her little sister helped paint her face and body
and put on her antler headdress.

She carried a bow and arrow
in honor of the brave hunters.
The dance began.
Powhatan was proud of his daughter.

Pocahontas' Uncle

Opechancanough, the brother of Powhatan, was very wise.
He spoke of things Pocahontas and her brothers had never seen.
Of tall ships, driven by the wind.
Of men with white faces and golden hair who carried sticks
that spat fire. He told them the story their grandfathers had told,
that strangers from across the sea would come and destroy
their people.

The boys were afraid.

Pocahontas saw their fear. So did Opechancanough.

"What do you think, Pocahontas?" he asked.

"I am not afraid," she said.

"I want to see the tall ships and the men with golden hair."

The Meeting

That spring the white men came to Powhatan's land.
The great chief sent scouts to watch them.
After much time, he and his men talked about the strangers.
There were many questions, but no answers.

The holy men began to chant and dance.
They called on their god Okewas to guide them.
Pocahontas watched. She thought about the strangers.
"I must see the white men," she said to her brother.
"Tomorrow I will follow the scouts' trail and find them."

The Strangers

By mid-morning Pocahontas had run a long way.
At the edge of a clearing she stopped to rest.
She heard voices. Quickly she hid.
She saw men. They had white faces. They were the strangers.
The one who seemed to be their leader began pointing.
The others started to cut down trees.
Pocahontas watched.
Then, without warning, a rabbit hopped in front of her.

The leader turned and looked in her direction.
Pocahontas held her breath. She didn't move.
Finally, the stranger looked away.
Slowly, Pocahontas crept back into the forest.

John Smith

Not long after, one of the strangers was captured
and taken to Powhatan's village.
Everyone went to the longhouse to see him.
Pocahontas stared. He was the leader,
the man from the clearing.
Holy men surrounded the stranger.
They shook their gourds in his face.
They shouted at him.

Two braves dragged the stranger before Powhatan.
They raised their war clubs.
Suddenly, Pocahontas ran to the stranger
and put her arms around him.
Powhatan looked at his daughter.
Then he spoke.
"Pocahontas has decided.
The stranger will live."

At Jamestown

The strangers were sick and starving.
They had not brought enough supplies from England.
They had not learned to plant corn.
Pocahontas begged her father to send them food.
Finally Powhatan agreed, and sent his daughter with baskets of corn, fish, and meat.
All winter Pocahontas brought food to the white men's fort.
Their leader, John Smith, became her friend.
He gave her gifts and told her stories.

He spoke of England, of kings and queens and princesses.
When Pocahontas heard these stories, she dreamed
of the day she would meet the English king.
Then she would wear her copper headband and tell him
about her people.
Of how they had saved the English from starving.
But most of all she would tell the English king about her
father, the great Chief Powhatan, ruler of all the
river tribes.

Drawing America

You can draw Pocahontas and her people, the Powhatan Indians. On the next few pages we have drawn pictures for you to copy and color. Copy the drawings freehand — or use the guidelines we've drawn. Here's how:

1. Copy the guidelines — the empty boxes. Ours are blue to make them easier to see. You can use a pencil and ruler.

2. Draw the main outlines of the figure, copying the lines in one box at a time.

3. Next add the details, like those on the arms, legs, face, and clothes. Remember to copy one box at a time.

Here's an idea for a simple tabletop display. Turn a box on its side. Draw a log fence — like the one built around Jamestown — on the back of the box. Tape cutout figures of Pocahontas and Captain John Smith to the side of the box. Put in as many figures as you like.

4. Erase the boxes.

5. Now you are ready to color. We used colored pencils on this picture. But you can use anything you like — pencils, watercolors, washable markers, or crayons.

Before the arrival of Europeans, Native Americans used animal skins for much of their clothing. Deerskin was probably the most popular for everyday use. It was often decorated with seashells, bones, porcupine quills and paint. Powhatan Indians also used body paints to decorate themselves.

Hollow gourds filled with pebbles make a lot of noise. Indian holy men used them in their religious rituals and dances. Snakeskins stuffed with grass made a fierce-looking headdress. Necklaces of bear claws and mountain lion claws were also common. The holy man's tunic was made from rabbit hides sewn closely together.

Native Americans who lived on the east coast of North America did not have metal tools or weapons. Instead, they used stones and pieces of bone. It took great skill to chip a small sharp arrowhead out of a stone.

This picture shows English settler Captain John Smith wearing a metal breastplate and helmet. He is carrying a musket.

Watercolors and colored pencils were used to color these pictures.

To build a longhouse, the Indians first made a frame of bent branches and small trees. Then they covered the frame with mats woven from marsh grasses. These mats could be rolled upwards to let in light and air. They could also be carried to other places when the tribe went on the winter hunt. Large flat pieces of bark were often used as coverings on smaller houses.

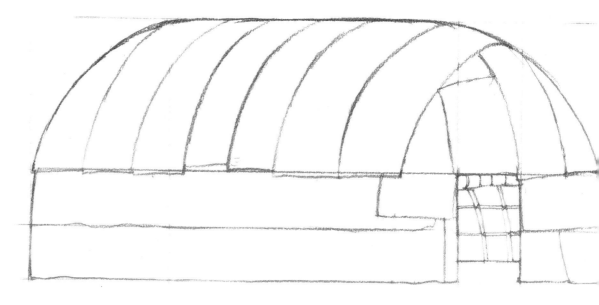

People of the river tribes used dugout canoes for fishing, traveling, and trading. The canoes were half-logs hollowed out by a combination of burning and scraping. Poles were used to move the dugouts. The river tribes used two-pronged spears, nets, and funnel-shaped traps made from reeds to catch many kinds of fish. They also collected shellfish and used the shells to make "wampum" beads, a form of money.

Indian men often wore mountain lion skins, complete with the tail.

Watercolors and colored pencils were used to color these pictures.

Powhatan was the *mamanatowick*, or "great chief," of all the river tribes. In this picture his headdress, called a "roach," is made of dyed deer hair. His headband is copper, as is the chest ornament. The deerskin is embroidered with tiny seashells. His robe is made of raccoon skins.

In this drawing, Pocahontas' mother wears a bone-and-shell headband and necklace. Her face and neck decorations are tattoos, but the decorations on her arms and legs are painted on. She is carrying a gourd for water and a carved wooden ladle.

Here is Pocahontas in her antler headdress and bear-claw necklace.

Watercolors and colored pencils were used to color these pictures. The same technique was used to do the illustrations for the story of Pocahontas.

A Note from the Authors

Did Pocahontas ever get her wish to visit England and meet the King? Yes. In 1613, Pocahontas was captured by the English and held for ransom. While she was a prisoner in Jamestown, Virginia, she met John Rolfe, an English settler. They fell in love and were married.

Three years later, Pocahontas (now christened Rebecca), John Rolfe, and their little son Thomas sailed to England for a visit. Pocahontas, the Princess of Powhatan, finally met the King of England. And she did tell him about her people.

As Pocahontas and her family were about to return to America, she fell ill and died. She is buried in England.

An Historical Footnote

The only written record of John Smith's capture and rescue appears in John Smith's personal journal.